Folk Magic

A Beginner's Guide to Time-Honoured Rituals, Spells and Customs

Lydia Levine

summersdale

FOLK MAGIC

Copyright © Octopus Publishing Group Limited, 2026

All rights reserved.

Text by Chris Turton

No part of this book may be reproduced by any means, nor transmitted, nor translated into a machine language, without the written permission of the publishers.

Condition of Sale
This book is sold subject to the condition that it shall not, by way of trade or otherwise, be lent, resold, hired out or otherwise circulated in any form of binding or cover other than that in which it is published and without a similar condition including this condition being imposed on the subsequent purchaser.

An Hachette UK Company
www.hachette.co.uk

Summersdale Publishers
Part of Octopus Publishing Group Limited
Carmelite House
50 Victoria Embankment
LONDON
EC4Y 0DZ
UK

This FSC® label means that materials and other controlled sources used for the product have been responsibly sourced

www.summersdale.com

The authorized representative in the EEA is Hachette Ireland, 8 Castlecourt Centre, Dublin 15, D15 XTP3, Ireland (email: info@hbgi.ie)

Printed and bound in Malaysia

ISBN: 978-1-83799-771-8
eISBN: 978-1-83799-772-5

Substantial discounts on bulk quantities of Summersdale books are available to corporations, professional associations and other organizations. For details contact general enquiries: telephone: +44 (0) 1243 771107 or email: enquiries@summersdale.com.

Disclaimer
Neither the author nor the publisher can be held responsible for any injury, loss or claim – be it health, financial or otherwise – arising out of the use, or misuse, of the suggestions made herein.

Contents

4	Introduction
6	A Word of Caution
8	Love and Relationships
32	Fortune and Success
56	Rewilding Yourself
80	Health and Well-Being
104	Lucky Charms
128	Folk Celebrations and Festivals
152	Conclusion
154	Notes

Introduction

Welcome to the enchanting world of folk magic! This age-old practice is deeply rooted in the quirks and tendencies of ordinary people who, centuries ago, turned to magical understanding – coupled with the use of humble, everyday items to focus their intent – to cure ailments, ward off malevolent spirits and advance themselves in love and fortune. As such, folk magic is as diverse and far-reaching as the human population, and indeed – just like folklore – it can be seen in a host of fascinating varieties in cultures across the world.

Because folk magic is so closely linked to the past, this book will offer a glimpse into the history of a particular practice, along with any associated folk tradition, while revealing exciting ways of applying it to your own present situation. Unlike high or ceremonial magic, folk magic is defined by its accessibility to all. In this

way, although there is a rich tapestry of established practices to consider, you are encouraged to develop your own methods and approaches. As with any magical practice, the aim is to direct your energies towards your goal and, in that respect, folk magic can be as unique as you are!

This book is intended as a waypost for curious beginners keen to explore this very personal and human practice. If you approach it with constructive intent, your heart and mind will be enriched by the wealth of wisdom it has to offer.

A Word of Caution

When using fire, candles, smudge sticks or water in your spells, always prioritize safety. Never leave flames unattended, keep safety principles in mind around open water – especially if there are young children or animals nearby – and ensure candles are placed on heat-resistant surfaces.

The diversity and relative simplicity of the practices collected under the banner of folk magic are perhaps its biggest appeal. It doesn't require privileged access to ancient texts or initiation into a protected group or the acquisition of obscure paraphernalia – it's extraordinary in its ordinariness! But, as we have hinted, folk magic – being "of the people" – is inextricably linked to specific eras and cultures, many of which are long-forgotten, some of which are alive and well.

While variations of similar ideas and practices can be found across the world in numerous periods, and the precise origins of a given charm or spell might be hazy at best, it is advised that anyone wishing to use the knowledge in this book should first familiarize themselves with the cultural history of the practice before proceeding. Of course, this book will go some way to providing this background, but the deeper your understanding of the world that gave rise to this humble art, the more potent your magic will be. This is the beauty of folk magic – not only a fascinating way to navigate the ups and downs of modern life but also an enlightening journey into the past.

As ever, it is advised that practitioners use their magic with honourable intentions and a keen awareness of karmic law.

Love and Relationships

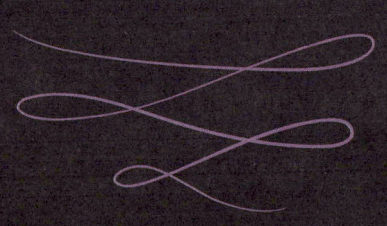

The pursuit of romance and the mending of familial rifts are things that most people experience at some point in their lives, and ever since matters of the heart have been perplexing us, everyday items have played a role. Whether it's plucking petals to the rhyme of "They love me, they love me not" or trying to decipher initials in the shape of a curled-up piece of apple peel, people have turned to folk traditions as a kind of giddy amusement. However, when we fold magic into the mix, the old ways offer uniquely sincere and personal approaches that can give more definite insights.

Magic will find those with pure hearts, even when all seems lost.

MORGAN RHODES

A HEART FULL OF LOVE IS AN UNSTOPPABLE FORCE

An incantation to detect true love

Romantic relationships are a wonderful blessing, but undoubtedly there are times when the bonds between two people are stressed, perhaps casting a shadow of doubt over the strength of the commitment. Ever since Venus, the Roman goddess of love, was associated with fruit, apples have played a significant role in European love magic, mostly as a means of divination, and this simple incantation can be used to tell if your love is true.

You will need:
- An apple

Performing the incantation:
This incantation should be performed on Easter morning. While eating the apple, speak aloud the following words:

> *As Eve in her thirst for knowledge ate,*
> *So, I too thirst to know my fate.*

Take care not to eat the core and, once you've finished, remove all the seeds from the fruit. If you find an odd number of seeds, it's a sign that your love will not last; if you find an even number of seeds, you can rest assured

that your relationship is destined to thrive. Of course, there are many non-magical ways to address marital tensions, so if you receive a disappointing result, use it as motivation to act constructively.

A charm to find love

The pursuit of romantic love is a deep-seated desire for many and has been expressed in magic for centuries, stretching as far back as the ancient Egyptians. In a post-industrial world, where modern technology connects people globally, the chances of finding a suitable partner are surely at their highest; but in bygone eras devoid of the joys of online dating apps, it's no wonder people appealed for a little outside assistance. This simple charm originated in Jersey, an island in the English Channel, and dates back to the early 1900s. It's a quaint way to determine who that special person might be.

You will need:

- A pair of shoes

Casting the spell:

This charm is intended for bedtime. When you're ready to sleep, take your shoes and place them under your bed, directly beneath your pillow, arranged in a "T" shape.

Once in bed, speak the following words aloud:

*I've put my shoes in the form of a T,
Hoping my true love to see,
Let them be young, or let them be old,
Let them come and visit me.*

A vision of your true love will appear in your dreams.

A spell to strengthen a friendship

A loyal and trustworthy friend should be cherished, and the importance of this kind of personal relationship has found iterations in countless folk customs. From showing one's tongue to a new acquaintance in Tibet to the pressing of noses (the *hongi*) in the Māori culture, these actions are all designed to acknowledge and reinforce the virtues of friendship. These old traditions – being performative and somewhat ritualistic – are magical in their own right, but if your aim is to strengthen a bond at the deepest level, this spell will be useful.

You will need:

- A pen or pencil
- Two pieces of plain letter-sized paper
- A needle and thread
- Two freshly cut flowers (one for you and one for your friend)
- A large, heavy book

Casting the spell:

Write the name of your friend 13 times on both pieces of paper. Pick up the flower you have selected for them, focus on it and imagine that your friend is emerging from the petals. As you're doing this, recite the following words:

*By stem and petal, leaf and bud,
Unfolding flower, I name you:
[speak the name of your friend].*

Place the flower between the two pieces of paper you've written on and lay them inside your heavy book to press them a little. Next, remove the sheets – with the pressed flower in between them – and sew the edges together while saying the following:

*Friends through thick and
friends through thin.*

Store the sewn packet in a safe place to preserve it.

FOR ADDED MAGIC…

Choose your friend's favourite flower
– or their birth flower – to make
the spell even more personal.

A spell to rekindle a lost romance

The complexities of modern life are such that two people in love can be separated unduly, yet deep-running sentiments are hard to dismiss. While the use of magic to force the hand of Cupid is not advised – since imposing your will so strongly on an unsuspecting person is likely to invite bad karma – if your heart yearns to reconnect with someone with whom you once shared a true connection, this spell can be used to open up the possibility. Although the charm used here is pure old folk magic, the spell does require a specific incense.

You will need:

- Dragon's blood incense (or dragon's blood resin)
- Matches or a lighter

Casting the spell:

Place the incense/resin in front of you, keeping it close. Light it and give it a chance to softly envelop you with its powerful aroma. With the name of your lost love in your mind, repeat the following words:

Dragon's blood, dragon's blood,
'Tis not your blood I wish to burn,
But my true love's heart I wish to turn.
May they never sleep, rest nor happy be,
Until they come or is sent to me.

MAGIC ALTERNATIVES...

Incense – loose or in stick form – is the easiest way to burn dragon's blood. However, if this is not available and you happen to have an open fire in your home, you can use salt. On three successive Friday nights, throw a little salt into the fire while using the same chant but omitting the first line and replacing "your blood" with "this salt".

Curious marriage customs

What we won't do for love? It's universally acknowledged that matters of the heart can lead to a kind of delirious affliction, where practically nothing is too much to appease the object of one's affection. This certainly seems the case when it comes to some of the curious and downright baffling customs that have emerged through the ages around the world. Take, for example, the Scottish tradition of the "blackening" of the bride (or groom, or both), which entails the couple being accosted and ceremonially humiliated by being pelted with messy material – be it rotten eggs, treacle or any other disagreeable substance – in front of their friends and family. This chaotic assault is designed to mentally prepare the victims for the kind of turmoil they might experience in married life. It is thought that the tradition began in the early nineteenth century, though the original version was a ceremonial cleansing rather than a humiliating soiling!

Speaking of waste matter, the Tidong people of Borneo have a unique way of ensuring that newlyweds are blessed in their union. After the big event, the couple are supervised to ensure they refrain from using the toilet for three days. This is because it is thought that, aside from being the source of an occasional bad smell, toilets can be harbingers of bad luck.

In a more savoury show of affection, "jumping the broom" (where bride and groom leap over an old-fashioned broom) has been observed in several cultures, from Welsh Romani ceremonies to African American unions. There is a complex history behind the practice, but in the latter case it signified a formal commitment in the absence of a civil ceremony.

A spell to mend familial rifts

Family bonds can be the most enduring connections we experience in life: the unwavering love of a parent can be lifesaving, and the companionship of a sibling built through childhood is priceless. The concept of family is also extremely important in folklore and customs. The transfer of knowledge particular to a given group, and pride in preserving it, from one generation to the next, is the essence of folk tradition. But our relations are only human after all, and just as likely to err and argue as anyone else. This highly personal spell will help bring them back together.

You will need:

- A small jar with a lid
- A candle
- 2 tbsp verbena (also known as vervain – this purple flower can be foraged or acquired as a powder)
- 1 tbsp dried camomile
- 1 tbsp dried lavender

Casting the spell:

Lay the items out in front of you and light the candle. Add the herbs/powder to the jar and, while doing so, say some words of your own about healing to declare

your intention – for example, "May all family ties be restored once more."

Screw the lid onto the jar and drip some wax from the candle around the edges to form a seal.

Store the jar in the family home or take it with you to any family meetings you might attend.

A chant to invoke joy

Any kind of relationship – whether it be with friends, family, colleagues or a significant other – will face challenges and be tested at times. Anything of value takes work to maintain, and while you can do your best to keep love, kindness and humility in your heart there may be days when your reserves are running low. This cheerful chant (which is really a short song) is from old Hebridean lore and has the same colourful, carefree feeling as "Que Será, Será" and is a kind of blessing for the past, present and future. Let its whimsical words lift your spirits and help you share positive energy with those you care for.

You will need:
- A clear throat and an enthusiastic tone

Performing the chant:
Simply recite the following words to invoke good vibes:

Cantil o, Cantil ee!
Joy to all thee gone before
Whose longer stay had pleased us.
Cantil o, Cantil ee!
Joy to all thee left behind
Whose leaving would have grieved us.
Cantil o, Cantil ee!
Joy to all thee still to come

Whose song may lift the weary.
Cantil o, Cantil ee!

FOR ADDED MAGIC…

Try to sing the words to a tune that feels in keeping with the cheerful spirit of the lines.

A spell to stop gossip

Words have immense power and are, of course, central to all magic. Words spoken in anger, spite or mischief are naturally loaded with destructive energy, and even when aimed indirectly at another person they can be detrimental. Of course, words are also the remedy to ill will and talking through any issues you might have should always be the first resort. However, if you find that civility is not winning out, this spell might help to change things for the better. It requires a red candle, the colour of which is associated with defence, and cloves, which are known to repel negative energy.

You will need:
- A handful of whole cloves
- A red candle in a holder
- A lighter or matches

Casting the spell:

First, it's necessary to prepare the candle by studding it with the cloves. To do this, apply a flame from a lighter or match to a spot on the candle to soften the wax – don't hold it too close or you will melt the candle. Once the wax is soft, push a clove into it. Repeat this until your candle is peppered with a dozen or so cloves.

Next, light the candle, picture the person who is directing the harmful words your way and say:

Speak no evil, write no ill,
May the tongue and hands be still.
As I bind, this is my will.

Let the candle burn out and the spell is done.

A spell for letting go of the past

Many people are now aware of the idea of living "in the now", fully immersing oneself in the present, free from distractions, to truly appreciate the infinite wonder and preciousness of existence. While this is a supremely worthy exercise, it can be hard to achieve when the weight of the past is keenly felt. As such, a little magical assistance might be required. Fire has always been associated with purification and transition, and one such example can be found in the old tradition of the Yule log. Most will know it simply as a chocolate cake eaten at Christmas, but its origins lie in the Old Norse festival of Jól, wherein a large log was burned to celebrate the rebirth of the sun during the winter solstice.

You will need:

- A candle in a holder
- A handful of marjoram, fresh or dried
- A pen and piece of paper
- A lighter or matches
- A fireproof dish

Casting the spell:

Place the candle and the fireproof dish in front of you.

Take a pinch of marjoram and sprinkle it around the candle in an anticlockwise direction (this motion is associated with repelling).

On the piece of paper, write down the things you're trying to let go of, then sprinkle some marjoram over the paper and fold it up into a little packet.

Light the packet from the flame of the candle and quickly drop it into your dish. Imagine a weight is being lifted as the smoke rises.

Extinguish the candle.

The folkish roots of Valentine's Day

Romantic love has long had an association with otherworldly forces. In Shakespeare's *A Midsummer Night's Dream*, which takes place mostly in a bewitching woodland realm bursting with life both natural and supernatural, fairy folk and humankind become entangled. Oberon, king of the fairies, creates a love potion made from a real-life flower, aptly called love-in-idleness – better known as wild pansy. Clearly Shakespeare himself was familiar with the folklore attached to this plant and its common association with Cupid, the Roman god of desire and erotic love.

Indeed, some scholars maintain that Valentine's Day has its roots in ancient Rome, derived from the pagan fertility festival known as Lupercalia. This event was observed annually on 15 February (not 14 February, which is when the modern-day iteration is celebrated) and featured one particular rite that involved naked

Luperci (priests of the Brotherhood of the Wolf) galloping anticlockwise around a hill, whipping people with goat-skin thongs as a kind of blessing. Women who wanted to conceive presented themselves to the Luperci in the hope that being struck by the whip might aid pregnancy.

Though the goat-skin whips have been left behind, some parts of the world celebrate the spirit of Valentine's Day as a time of plenty, even today. In areas of Norfolk, in the East of England, the Santa-Claus-like figure of Jack Valentine has been known to steal out into the night, place a small gift at the door of deserving folk and knock before disappearing.

Like so many modern-day celebrations and traditions, Valentine's Day has a rich and diverse history infinitely more interesting and sincere than the compulsory exchanging of saccharine greetings cards and chocolates. Why not celebrate next year in a more folky way, on 15 February, or start your own tradition inspired by the past?

Fortune and Success

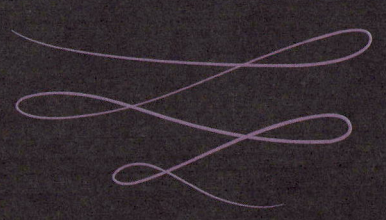

The desire to prosper and connect with a sense of worthiness is universal – however, what form your prosperity might take is something that is unique to you. You might see success as financial security and the accumulation of material goods or take the more enlightened approach and simply strive to be the best possible version of yourself. Most of us will aim for a little of both. Folk customs to encourage good fortune occur across the world – from the tradition of always gifting a new wallet with a coin inside to displaying a lucky *maneki-neko* (the "beckoning cat" in Japanese culture) in your home or place of work. Whatever your goal, the key is learning, through magical practice, to harmonize your intent with the free-flowing, ever-changing forces of the universe, which will help you perceive a fruitful outcome in any situation.

Fate leads him who follows it,
and drags him who resists.

PLUTARCH

STAY FOCUSED, BE FREE

A bay-leaf blessing for manifestation

Being an evergreen shrub, bay has long been regarded as having special properties – its dense, deep-green leaves are plentiful throughout the seasons, and it represents health, wealth and abundance. In magic, bay has a particular association with wish fulfilment and can help you manifest something specific. For this spell it's necessary to burn your bay leaves, so it's recommended that you acquire what you need (one for each manifestation you wish to make) and, if fresh, dry them in an airy spot inside until brittle.

You will need:
- Bay leaves (one for each manifestation)
- A marker pen
- A candle in a holder
- A fireproof dish
- A lighter or matches

Performing the blessing:

Begin by lighting the candle and positioning the fireproof dish nearby.

With the marker pen, write a word that represents your wish on the leaf (you won't have room to be much more precise).

Taking one at a time, light the bay leaves while saying the following words:

Bay, grant me the wisdom to know what to do in order to make my wishes come true.

Once the leaf is alight, drop it into the dish.

Collect the ash once cooled and fold it up into a paper packet. Place the packet underneath your pillow so you'll dream of ways to make your wishes come true.

A charm to assist in acquiring a house or land

Moving house is one of life's more mundane trials. It involves a lot of paperwork, financial expense and organization, which can add up to quite a bit of stress. Of course, once the ordeal is over, you can begin to make that house or plot your sanctuary, and all the effort seems worthwhile – but this takes time and, seemingly, a bit of luck. One of the most testing aspects is landing the house or plot you're aiming for, and it often seems like chance has a role to play. This old English charm offers a quirky way to help you in your quest.

You will need:
- A packet of leek seeds

Performing the charm:
To avoid any misgivings from the owner of the house or land, this charm is best carried out during an arranged viewing of the property.

With the seeds in your hand as you walk the boundary of the plot, drop one every so often, making sure you cover the entire perimeter.

With luck, you will be successful in your acquisition – though you may have to deal with a few random sprouting alliums down the line!

A prosperity bowl for good fortune

In Chinese culture, the concept of "like attracts like" is well established – whether it be cash coins hung on a red cord or jade charms carved in the shape of a dragon. This is the idea behind the prosperity bowl, in which you collect objects of monetary and personal value to attract more of the same.

You will need:

- A bowl large enough to contain the items you'll be adding to it (ideally, choose a bowl that is gold- or silver-coloured)
- Items that you associate with material wealth, as well as those that will attract positive energies in the magical context, such as:
  - Cash, coins or paper money
  - Herbs/spices, such as cinnamon sticks, star anise, mint and basil
- A candle (ideally green, but white will do)
- Any other object that represents prosperity to you
- A bundle of dried sage for smudging
- A fireproof dish (that will fit in the bowl alongside the other items)
- A lighter or matches

Casting the spell:

To begin, light the sage bundle and cleanse your bowl with its smoke.

Add each of the items to the bowl. As you do, concentrate on their significance to connect them to your intention.

Place the fireproof dish in the centre of the bowl, set the candle securely on top and light it.

Once the candle has burned out, place the bowl in the rear-left corner of your home (this spot is related to prosperity in feng shui).

A marigold bath to enhance your confidence and acclaim

One of the key elements to success is confidence. Not only does this give you faith in your own abilities – and so removes any subconscious hurdles that might trip you up in your endeavour – it gives the impression that you're capable and in charge. If you seem like you're in control, people are more likely to put their trust in you. But feeling confident can sometimes be a challenge, especially when you're venturing into new territory. This simple ritual featuring the humble marigold, which has strong associations with the sun, will cleanse and energize, giving you a bright, irresistibly likeable disposition.

You will need:

- A handful of marigold petals, fresh or dried
- A yellow candle (yellow is associated with confidence, self-worth and positivity)

Performing the ritual:

Start by running a warm bath.

Take the petals and sprinkle them onto the water. As you do so, recite the following words:

*By the magic in this flower
show to all my inner power.*

Next, light the candle and, as you do so, say:

*By the magic in this flame
I will be held in great acclaim.*

Slip into the bath and absorb the warm, positive energy.

Once you're done, as you're stepping out, recite a final intention:

*Worthy and virtuous let me be,
respect and admiration flow to me.*

A spell to improve your finances

As the old saying goes, "Money makes the world go round" – which is another way of saying money is a means to most practical ends. While the pursuit of material wealth over personal enrichment will always be misguided, the reality of everyday life in most places across the world demands a certain amount of financial exchange. As stated in the introduction to this chapter, prosperity magic is best used to open one's eyes to opportunities that can be acted upon rather than to make cash materialize in your wallet! So, this spell will be most effective if you're embarking on a new financial venture.

You will need:

- A candle
- A dried four-leaf clover (a paper one will do if you can't get hold of a real one)
- A coin (preferably a nice, shiny new one)
- A fireproof dish
- A lighter or matches

Casting the spell:

Light the candle and have the fireproof dish nearby.

Flip the coin until it lands on "heads" three times in a row (this might take some patience but be persistent!).

Once you've hit your lucky streak, take the four-leaf clover and set it alight with the candle, dropping it quickly into the fireproof dish. As it smoulders, focus your intent.

Let the candle burn out and the spell is complete.

FOR ADDED MAGIC…

Choose a green, gold or silver candle, as these colours are associated with good fortune.

A spell for success in a new enterprise

Embarking upon a new enterprise – be it a business venture, a learning opportunity or a romantic pursuit – will always involve a degree of risk. Of course, it's possible (and advisable!) to assess the pitfalls that might be involved and prepare yourself to deal with them, but you should also recognize the role that good fortune can play. The key is to focus on success as much as possible, but this spell can boost your chances by attracting some prosperous energy.

You will need:

- A handful of blue alkanet flowers (this plant is common in gardens but can also be foraged in wildflower meadows and verges)
- Two squares of fabric, roughly 10 cm x 10 cm (4 in. x 4 in.)
- A needle and green thread

Casting the spell:

First, create a pocket with the squares of fabric. Pin them together and sew around three edges.

Place your flowers inside and recite the following words:

May this project be blessed with success for me, with love and gratitude so mote it be.

Sew the remaining side of the square to seal the pouch.

Have the pouch with you whenever your activities relate to the project at hand.

Chinese prosperity traditions

China has a fascinating and intricate culture of tradition, which is deeply rooted in ancestral customs and still a part of everyday life for many. To describe these practices as folklore would be to underestimate their prevalence and significance, but many of the well-worn traditions kept alive today originate from a time when belief in mythical creatures, a host of gods and supernatural forces was commonplace.

Customs related to health, wealth and prosperity abound in China, many of which are centred around the Spring Festival, which celebrates the New Year according to the lunisolar Chinese calendar. Aside from the festival providing an opportunity for families to get together and share in good cheer, symbolic customs

are enacted to help ensure that the coming year is a fruitful one. The gifting of money in decorative red envelopes *(hong bao)* to children at this time is, naturally, a warmly welcomed gesture, but it's also a way of warding off negative energies; *ya sui qian*, the Chinese term for the "lucky money" inside the envelopes, also means "money to keep off evil spirits".

Another Spring Festival tradition is that of the New Year picture *(nianhua)*, an art print hung at this time to inspire prosperous thoughts for the year ahead. The original subject of these works was that of the door gods of the Han Dynasty, but modern incarnations depict all kinds of celebratory symbols, such as birds, flowers and ploughing cattle.

An altar for abundance

Although the idea of an altar leans more towards ceremonial magic, having a fixed space that makes focusing your intent easier is always beneficial. Altars typically include candles, totems of magical significance or specific symbols, a place for burning incense, as well as crystals and, often, a plant of some kind. To keep your altar more within the folk bracket, it's better to use household and garden items; anything that is traditionally associated with good luck and prosperity will suit, including items you have found to be helpful in this regard. Below is a spell that will help specifically with attracting abundance.

You will need:

- A few fresh basil leaves (associated with money)
- A few dried bay leaves (associated with wish fulfilment and success)
- A pinch of dried thyme (for business success)
- A few sprigs of clover (for luck and happiness)
- A few flowers, a piece of fruit or a vegetable, ideally harvested from your garden

Casting the spell:

Select a spot indoors for your altar – a surface that you can sit in front of comfortably and which won't be disturbed by pets. (To ensure your altar remains

coherent and your items stay together, you could use a tray or shallow box.)

Arrange the basil, bay, thyme and clover in a way that seems fitting to you, leaving a space for the vegetables, etc., to be placed.

Set out the harvested produce on your altar, focus on the bounty that it represents and say aloud:

> *As the season yields its bounty, I give thanks and know that my own hopes and dreams will bring a rich harvest.*

A spell for charming personal items

When facing a daunting situation, such as a job interview, a first date or a medical appointment, a little extra confidence can go a long way. A simple and discreet way to achieve this is to charm a cherished personal item, such as a piece of jewellery, a hairpin or anything else that you can carry or wear easily. Charming is about imbuing an item with a particular energy that can be utilized by the carrier. It's helpful if the item in question has established associations with the intent that it's being used for (e.g. a gold ring for prosperity), but the most important thing is that you're able to make strong associations of your own when you're charming.

You will need:

- A small (ideally wearable or easily portable) personal item
- A quiet space to charm the object

Performing the charm:

Ensure that you're sitting in a quiet, undisturbed space so you can focus without distraction.

Hold your chosen object, visualize whatever you want the object to represent and feel your energy

transferring to it. To help with this, you could even speak your intention to the object or vocalize an affirmation that sums up what the item will provide impetus for.

Wear or carry your item whenever you need to draw on its power.

FOR ADDED MAGIC...

Recite the affirmation you used to charm the object each time you wear or carry it.

A good harvest and a merry May in the UK

Many of the curious folk customs in Europe are related to encouraging prosperity in the context of the approaching season. Since most of these practices were established at a time when the majority of people's livelihoods centred around food, a great deal of them focus on ensuring a bountiful crop of one sort or another. Take, for example, the English tradition of orchard wassailing, which takes place in winter, in early January. The ceremony, which arose from the cider-producing counties, was undertaken to encourage a hearty apple crop. Still performed to this day (also by those who are simply keen to be involved in some old-world fun), it involves beating the largest tree in the orchard with sticks to scare off any evil spirits that might be lurking, the hanging of toasted bread from the tree's branches (food for the guardians of the apple tree, the robin) and the reciting of

traditional songs. The word "wassail" is derived from the Saxon *waes haeil*, meaning "good health", so, naturally, there is also plenty of ale and cider involved.

In the spring, when nature is beginning to bud and bloom, there is cause for celebration. One age-old custom found across Europe – in the UK, Scandinavia and Germany especially – is that of the maypole. Each region has its local variation, but the general idea is that, on 1 May (midsummer in some countries), a tall pole decorated with garlands is erected on communal ground as the focus of a spring celebration. In the UK, the festivities include a maypole dance, which involves long lengths of brightly coloured ribbon attached near the top of the pole, the ends of which are held by participant dancers. The troupe skip happily around the maypole to music until the ribbon is woven neatly around the pole.

Rewilding Yourself

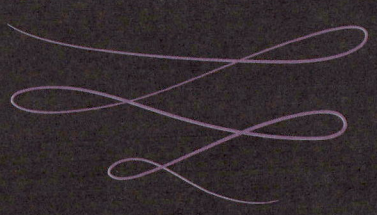

The idea of living in tune with nature and the seasons is an ancient one, born out of the practical necessity and innate desire to connect with the universal forces believed to shape people's fortunes. A lot of folk magic is based around herbology, a body of knowledge that was once much more commonplace than it is today. Being in tune with the ebb and flow of the growing seasons, and having knowledge of the local wildlife and a healthy respect for the land, was not only advantageous for the practice of magic but essential for day-to-day living. Today, we're tangled in an intricate web of data and hyperstimulation, and despite the infinite wealth of information at our fingertips, knowledge of self and our place in the world at large is obscured. Reconnecting with our natural surroundings and with elemental forces is something that can reawaken a deep sense of purpose and belonging – and can be enhanced through folk magic.

*Nature is the source of
all true knowledge.*

LEONARDO DA VINCI

FIND YOUR ROOTS AND YOU WILL FIND YOUR FUTURE

Fire scrying for divination

Although fire is not strictly a natural element, its transformative power and mesmerizing form make it an unbridled force akin to air or water. The discovery of fire played a pivotal role in humankind's evolution and, ever since, it has taken on profound symbolic significance in spiritual and magical thinking, with links to celestial bodies and the sun. One way it has been adopted into folk magic is through the art of fire scrying – that is, divination through the interpretation of images perceived in the flames. This practice will allow you to connect with the untamed spirit of the fire and illuminate your destiny. Poppy seeds are significant as they are believed to enhance psychic ability.

You will need:

- A handful of poppy seeds
- A fire, burning in a cauldron or hearth
- A notebook and pen

Casting the spell:

While sitting in front of the fire, hold the poppy seeds in your hand.

Concentrate on the subject you wish to receive a vision about and cast the seeds into the fire. (Be sure not to lean in too close afterwards, as your seeds may pop and fly out of the fire!)

Look into the flames and relax your eyes. If and when you catch a glimpse of an image or outline you recognize, write it down and consider what significance it might hold for you.

A feathered spell for manifestation

Birds have always been a symbol of hope – their freewheeling flight and ecstatic song lift our spirits and inspire us to dream of limitless horizons – and, of course, they have strong associations in folklore. Owls are famed for being wise and storks are fabled for delivering babies, and while such fancies might seem quaint and unbelievable, there's no denying that birds present a very familiar and relatable face of nature in our everyday lives. This spell takes interaction with our feathered friends a step further, trusting them to assist in manifesting something we might desire.

You will need:
- A photograph/picture representing what you want to manifest
- A small bag of wild bird seed
- A bowl
- A bottle of water

Casting the spell:
Head to a quiet woodland location and find a small clearing.

Set the photo/picture down on the ground and place the bowl on top of it. Fill the bowl with water from the bottle.

Take a handful of bird seed and spread it in a wide circle around the bowl.

Return to the location the next day and remove the bowl and picture.

With luck, the object of your desire will be manifested in two weeks. If not, consider trying again in a different spot.

A hag stone to connect with earth energy

Immersing yourself in the lush tranquillity of the great outdoors has long been considered a healing experience – and modern science has confirmed as much. Experiencing the wonders of nature in their infinite variety is an undeniable joy, yet we often overlook the fact that without the rich, nourishing soil the mighty oak couldn't grow, without the clay the winding river couldn't run and without the stone the majestic mountain couldn't stand. Connecting with the earth is a means of healing and strengthening yourself, and one way to do this is to acquire a hag stone. Often found on beaches, these small stones have been shaped by the elements, creating a hole right through them. Folklore describes their use as talismans of protection against the "hag spirit", which might bring nightmares, but aside from this protective use they can be used for healing and to enhance prosperity.

You will need:

- A hag stone

Casting the spell:

Find a quiet spot outdoors so that you can fully connect with the elements.

With the hag stone in your left hand, visualize yourself being healed, if that's your intention, or focus on something you wish to achieve. As you're doing so, rub the stone in a clockwise direction.

Keep the stone with you at all times and repeat the manifestation as you see fit.

Moon water for spell enhancement

The moon is one of the most important symbols in magic, having strong associations with motherhood, femininity and nurturing. Water, being essential to life on Earth, has a healing and cleansing energy, and when combined with the power of the moon it can make for a potent, magical tool. Using these two natural energies together will strengthen your relationship with the life-giving forces at work in the natural world and will help to enhance any spell you're hoping to cast. As ever, the phase of the moon will affect the properties of your water.

You will need:
- Purified (filtered) water
- A jar or vial
- A tag or label

Casting the spell:
Fill the jar or vial with the water and seal it tightly.

Next, place the container outside, where it will be exposed to moonlight (as well as taking note of the phase of the moon, you'll want to ensure the night is going to be clear of cloud cover).

The idea is to retrieve the water before the sun comes up, so set an alarm to help you.

Once you've collected the water, label it with the phase of the moon it was exposed to and store it in a cool, dry place away from sunlight.

The properties infused during the different phases are as follows:

- New moon – will help with new prospects
- Waxing moon – will enhance manifestation and prosperity
- Full moon – will generally strengthen any of your intentions
- Waning moon – will help with separation or banishment

Native American folklore

There are countless examples of cultures across the world that, rather than losing sight of nature amid an imposing wave of modernity, have managed to preserve a special relationship with it. One such group of cultures can be found in the First Nation people of North America, who, despite having intricate regional differences, are united in a reverence for the natural world. Essentially, they see themselves as fully integrated with nature, regarding plants and animals not only as allies but also as kin, neither above nor below their own order.

This concept permeates many aspects of Native American life and is expressed in their folklore, which is often based on an oral tradition of storytelling. Many narratives are united in their depiction of a Great Spirit – a benevolent, omnipresent force responsible for life on Earth. The close relationship with nature is expressed

through countless tales relating to a host of indigenous animals: the bear often symbolizes power, wisdom and healing; the wolf is another representation of power and courage; the eagle has links with the spirit world and the coyote is a trickster figure. The turtle is perhaps the most significant of all the animals when it comes to the concept of nature as the unifying force of existence. Many First Nation people believe that the planet rests on the back of a World Turtle – that the Earth is literally an extension of a giant shell. The Lenape and the Iroquois believe that the planet began as a pile of dirt on the back of a sea turtle that continued to grow until it supported the whole world.

A ritual to connect with Mother Earth

The idea of "Mother Earth" has been expressed in many cultures across the centuries. Gaia, in Greek mythology, was the ancestral mother of all life and the personification of Earth; for the Romans, it was Venus; and for the Incans, it was Pachamama who preserved the bounty of life on Earth. Almost everyone will be able to recognize, without too much effort, that the natural world is something to be cherished and admired, but establishing a more profound connection with Mother Earth will attune your senses and deepen your understanding of the creative, healing energy that exists all around you. As with many folk-magic approaches, this naturally involves the use of common flora.

You will need:

- Access to a living plant or herb with which you feel a connection (this could be a birth flower, a herb you use often or simply a plant you admire)

Performing the ritual:

Ideally while outdoors, caress the plant with both hands and attempt to sense its energy.

Next, picture your heart as a blooming flower with a warm light at its centre.

See the light flow from your heart and into the plant, extending to the tips of its leaves, down its stem and into its roots.

Give thanks to Mother Earth for her love and healing.

A tree sigil for healing or protection

Trees are one of nature's everyday miracles and are life-giving in so many ways. The magical significance of trees is ancient and varied, ranging from connections to the spirit world and cosmology to rebirth and protection. In this case, trees will serve as the inspiration for a sigil, the purpose of which will be determined by the tree you choose to work with. If your sigil is intended for protection, find a rowan or aspen; if you want healing, find an ash or spruce; use online sources or a book to help you identify which is which.

You will need:
- Access to a tree
- A pen/pencil and some paper

Creating the sigil:
Locate a tree suitable for your purposes and set your intention – focus on what it is you want the tree to help you with.

Next, appeal to the tree for its help, based on your intention. If you feel your request has not been well received, try another tree.

Once you feel you have connected with the tree, ask for its help in creating a sigil. Following this, observe the patterns in the bark to pick out a set of lines that seem to make a shape.

Copy or trace the shape you perceive onto the paper to obtain your tree sigil.

A charm to harness the power of the wind

You may be familiar with the phrase "the winds of change", and there are obvious reasons why this natural force is associated with transformation. In terms of weather, the wind has a regulatory effect, with the power to usher in a storm or redistribute heat across large distances. Our personal experience of the wind can be of its disruptive nature, but if we're looking for a transformative influence in our lives it can be very useful. While European sailors in the thirteenth century used wind knots for the practical purpose of summoning a gust when their sails were slack, it's possible to catch the wind to harness its energy when you need an emotional or physical boost.

You will need:

- A 30-cm (12-in.) length of small-gauge cord or rope
- A day where the wind can be felt keenly

Casting the spell:

Find a place outside to sit, settle your mind and focus on your breath. Notice your exhalations blending effortlessly with the wind.

Ask that the wind let you know when you should tie your knots and, with your length of cord in hand, wait until you feel the time is right.

At this moment, tie an overhand knot and recite the following words:

I ask that the power of the wind be placed in this knot for safekeeping.

Repeat these steps until you have three knots on your cord.

FOR ADDED MAGIC…

Head out to a hilltop or mountainside to increase your connection with the natural force of the wind. Be sure to keep your personal safety in mind when out on any elevated location.

A sun spell for closure

Without the warmth and light from our sun, the Earth would not be able to support life. It is the source and sustenance of everything living, and it brings us joy when we see it blazing in the sky. When we consider this, it's hard to imagine a more intimate relationship with a celestial body, and it's easy to see why, as early as the Neolithic period, people worshipped the sun, treating it as a god that needed to be revered and appeased. Today, though the most common form of sun worship involves a sandy beach and a bottle of factor 50, it's still possible to establish a bond with this most majestic of stars. In magic, the sun represents vitality, strength and renewal, the latter of which is the focus of this spell.

You will need:

- A yellow or orange candle
- A pen/pencil and a slip of paper for each thing you'd like to let go of
- A fireproof dish
- A lighter or matches

Casting the spell:

This spell should be cast at sunset, from a spot where you can see the sun either directly or through a window.

On each of the slips of paper, write down briefly what it is you'd like closure on.

Light the candle, set the slip of paper alight and drop it into the dish.

Repeat this step until all the slips of paper are burned.

To close, recite the following words:

*May my woes begone
With the setting of the sun.*

Extinguish the candle and watch the sun as it disappears.

The magic of mushrooms

Mushrooms have always had a strong association with magic and the otherworldly. You may remember the classic image of a fairy or perhaps a gnome perched on a toadstool as depicted in various children's storybooks, and indeed fungi folklore in Europe suggests that a circle of mushrooms – known as a fairy ring – is a spot where fairy folk are likely to gather. In Slavic folklore, the red-and-white-spotted fly agaric mushroom is connected to the horned deity of earth, water, livestock and the underworld, Veles, who is believed to have offered the mushroom as a gift to humans.

What science has to say about fungi is equally as compelling. Recent studies have found that the mycelial network (the underground web that is the source of the fruiting bodies) is not only vast compared to the fleshy tip of the

iceberg that is the mushroom itself but it is also used by trees to share nutrients with each other and even send information about encroaching diseases or pests.

And, of course, mushrooms have many magical significances too. The humble oyster mushroom, which emerges as a charming array of creamy brown flutes, often growing on wood, is linked to healing and protection. The alien-looking morel, with its deeply pitted, brain-like cap, can attract good fortune; while the lion's mane, shaped like a cascade of milky icicles, can help with clarity of vision. These and more have been used to enhance the spellwork of folk over the ages – but be aware that foraging for mushrooms requires a certain level of knowledge and, therefore, this activity is not recommended unless under the supervision of an expert.

Health and Well-Being

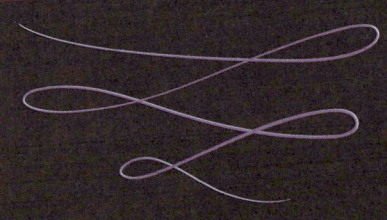

In many cultures throughout history, before the modern age of pharmaceutical medicine, the curing of common ailments was the business of the local healer. These people were incredibly important within their communities, as they would not only treat physical illness but could also offer magical remedies to help resolve spiritual matters. In the Americas, one might call this person a shaman; in Africa, a witch doctor; in Europe, a "cunning" man or woman. Naturally, their treatments were rooted in folk magic, utilizing their intricate knowledge of the local flora and fauna and the application of everyday items to bring about a positive outcome for those who employed their services. While many of these practices have been lost to time, traces persist; for example, some of us have been taught that the dock leaf will soothe a nettle sting and that rooibos will help with insomnia. This chapter presents a wealth of healing folk magic.

*Wellness encompasses
a healthy body,
a sound mind
and a tranquil spirit.*

LAURETTE GAGNON BEAULIEU

HEAL WITHOUT
AND HEAL WITHIN

An apple charm for curing all

"An apple a day keeps the doctor away," as the saying goes. While this old proverb isn't strictly about apples – rather the promotion of wellness through eating fruit and vegetables more generally – it's perhaps not entirely insignificant that the apple was chosen to represent good health. Some modern-day studies have revealed that eating an apple a day helps lower cholesterol and, statistically speaking, people who consume the fruit regularly are less likely to use prescription medicines in general. We've already made several mentions of apples in this book, and it seems that it might just be the most magical fruit available. Here's one way that it can be used as a cure-all.

You will need:
- An apple
- A sturdy, sterile pin

Casting the spell:
Take the pin (make sure it's a fairly heavy-gauge one) and sterilize it by dropping it into an inch or so of boiling water.

After the water has cooled, fish out the pin and dry it off.

Next, use the pin to scratch the following words into the skin of your apple:

Hax, pax, max, Deus adimax

Whoever it is that needs healing should then eat the apple.

A smoke stick for cleansing the home

The idea of "smudging" (cleansing a person or space by conducting a ceremony that involves burning sacred herbs) originated in Native American cultures and employs white sage specifically. While this ceremony should not be imitated by the uninitiated, smoke cleansing with herbs and incense has been practised widely outside of this tradition. As such, if you feel comfortable with the premise, creating and using your own smoke-cleansing stick in your home is a pleasant way to purify the space. Sage is associated with purification, wisdom and healing; rosemary with protection and clarity; and mint with attracting good luck and positive energy.

You will need:
- A dozen or so leafy stems of sage, mint or rosemary
- Plastic-free twine
- Scissors
- A lighter or matches

Casting the spell:
Collect the herb stems together in a bunch and bind them at the base with the twine (tie a knot with the loose end but keep the spindle end attached to the reel).

Wrap the spindle end up the length of the herbs at 2.5-cm (1-in.) intervals, cut the twine and tie off.

Hang the herb stick in an airy spot indoors to dry (this may take a week or so).

When the herbs are dry, the cleansing can begin. Take the stick and light the end using the lighter/matches. It should smoulder like incense.

Carry it through the house, allowing the purifying smoke to pervade a little before moving on.

Once you've covered every room, stub out the stick, which can be used in future cleansings.

A charm for a sore throat

Famously, it is said that there is no medical cure for the common cold, but numerous ways to treat the symptoms have been developed over the decades, particularly those of a sore throat. Honey, ginger, lemon, liquorice root, salt and apple cider vinegar have all been offered as ways to soothe the pain of a sore throat, and while any of these is surely worth a try, you might want to consider adding the following magical solution to your arsenal. It involves birch – long regarded as having purifying properties – which may be obtained online in the form of chips/shavings or can be carefully foraged. If foraging for birch, ensure you have a reliable way to identify the tree (the photo opposite will serve as a basic reference) and take a short piece of the thinnest woody limb. An alternative would be to shave a small piece of bark.

You will need:

- A small piece of birch wood

Casting the spell:

To relieve the pain, simply take the piece of birch and make the sign of the cross nine times over your throat.

FOR ADDED MAGIC...

Before using the charm, why not cleanse yourself with the herb stick mentioned on page 86? Simply light your stick and hold it near your midriff so the healing smoke can drift up towards your head.

Shamanic practices in South America

As mentioned at the outset of this chapter, many ancient cultures relied on a medicine man (though in Europe this role was often adopted by a woman) to cure ailments of the body as well as the spirit. This person, essentially the chief folk magician of the community, often combined natural remedies, passed down through generational knowledge, with traditional ceremonies. In some areas of the world these practices still exist, including among various indigenous peoples of South America.

In certain remote areas of the continent, indigenous communities, such as the Ona, the Yaghan and the Waimaha, have preserved their shamanic culture. Here the shaman is ultimately a spiritual locus and thus the source of sacred knowledge, often obtained through vision quests, which can be shared and interpreted for the benefit of the community. The vision quest often involves the shaman achieving an ecstatic state through the combination of hypnotic ritual performance and the ingestion of a natural hallucinogen. One such substance, which has become somewhat familiar in the West, is *yagé*, a liquid infusion that uses part of the *Banisteriopsis caapi* vine. Collective ceremonies involving *yagé* are organized for those seeking healing. Participants often undertake a series of preparatory measures designed to prepare the body, mind and spirit for the experience – limiting food and alcohol intake and perhaps ingesting certain cleansing herbs. The ceremony may also involve dancing, chanting and percussion. On a physical level, the *yagé* brew is supposed to expel toxins from the body (often when ingested it results in vomiting), and on a spiritual level it offers dream-like insight into anything that might be troubling the spirit. The shaman is at the centre of the ceremony and, as such, confirms their role as the chief health-giver.

A spell jar for attracting positive vibes

A spell jar, a modern take on what was referred to in Elizabethan England as a "witch bottle", is essentially a magnet for positive energy. The old ways dictate that the jar should be buried in the farthest corner of the home or otherwise secreted, but if it's visible it will remind you of its purpose and strengthen the resolve. This is another highly personal folk charm and, as such, can contain anything you associate with good luck, healing and good fortune.

You will need:

- A glass jar with a lid
- A sprig of rosemary or a pinch of the dried herb (to banish negativity)
- A sage leaf or a pinch of the dried herb (for wisdom)
- A few dried cloves (for protection)
- A shell (to represent water and going with the flow)
- A feather (to represent air and spiritual guidance)
- A stone (to represent earth and longevity)
- A coin (for wealth)
- A small bell (for good energy)
- A small candle (to represent light, warmth and fire)

Creating the spell jar:

Set out the jar and other items in front of you.

Place each item in the jar and, as you do, meditate on its significance.

Seal the jar and place in your chosen spot to start attracting that positive energy.

FOR ADDED MAGIC...

Add some of the magical items suggested in the Rewilding Yourself chapter, such as moon water (good for spell enhancement) or a hag stone (for protection).

An ancient charm for wellness

Many people will be familiar with this most magical of phrases: abracadabra. Unless you're well versed in the history of magic, you might have only heard this word as a prompt by a stage magician before they produce a bouquet of flowers from their hat or make their glamorous assistant miraculously reappear. Its precise origins are unknown, but it has been identified in the *Liber Medicinalis*, a medical text from the second century, relating to a cure for fever. As such, it's probably the oldest healing spell in existence. It has been adopted across centuries in a host of contexts – used by Roman emperors, by Gnostics, by Londoners trying to ward off the plague and by the prominent occultist Aleister Crowley. Needless to say, it has had an enduring impact, which attests to its popularity and power. The idea behind the triangular shape is that as the word diminishes on each subsequent line, so too will your ailment.

You will need:
- A small piece of paper
- A locket or a necklace with a sealable compartment

Creating the charm:

On the piece of paper, copy out the letters as shown below:

ABRACADABRA
ABRACADABR
ABRACADAB
ABRACADA
ABRACAD
ABRACA
ABRAC
ABRA
ABR
AB
A

Roll or fold up the paper as small as you can and place it inside your locket.

Wear the charm for as long as it takes for you to heal.

A charm for sound sleep

A good night's sleep is not just satisfying – scientific study has shown it to be essential to our well-being. Sleep allows the body to repair its tissues, regulate blood pressure and heart rate and strengthen our immune system. It's also crucial for our mental processes, from consolidating new information to reducing stress and improving mood. It's basically one of the most significant ways you can improve your physical and mental health. However, due to the stresses and strains of modern life, our sleep is often compromised. Whether it's the blue light from our phone screen telling our brain it's time to wake up when we're scrolling near bedtime or a lack of exercise prohibiting our body from slipping into a slumber more naturally, we're sleeping less comfortably than ever. This old English charm, using a humble pair of shoes, might just help you get your full 40 winks.

You will need:
- A pair of shoes

Performing the charm:
Prepare yourself for bed as usual. (You might want to improve your chances by refraining from any screen time at least an hour before.)

Take a pair of your shoes and, under where you sleep, arrange them side by side facing in opposite directions.

Your sleep will be interruption free, untroubled by nightmares or any other such disturbances.

A yarn spell for cleansing

Sometimes it's hard to pin down exactly what it is that's making you feel unwell. Everyday factors such as diet, exercise, sleep and your work-life balance are all areas to investigate and assess. However, if you feel you've done all you can and you still don't feel right, consider trying this simple spell. (This should be cast for the person who is feeling unwell by another person.)

You will need:
- A ball of red wool (here the red symbolizes the negative energy that will be removed)
- Scissors
- A lighter or matches
- A fireproof bowl

Casting the spell:

With the person who is feeling unwell standing in front of you, facing away, take the loose end of the ball of wool and have them hold it at their crown.

Unravel the wool until it reaches their heel.

Hold your finger at this point and ask the person to let go of the other end. Next, take one of the person's shoes and add that length to the measurement of wool you already have. Cut the length of wool at this point.

With the length of wool in your hand, recite the following words:

I cleanse [person's name] of any sickness or negativity – so mote it be.

Then place the wool into the fireproof bowl and burn it.

Once the wool has burned, take it to a place away from the person's property and bury it in the ground.

A sun meditation for increased energy

We've already covered the biological importance of the sun and how it's the primary source of life-giving energy on Earth, but of course it also has the power to revitalize the spirit. Most people are aware that sunlight imparts vitamin D, which can be difficult to obtain in the required quantity through diet alone. Exposure to the sun helps you to gain the necessary levels of this vitamin, essential for supporting your immune system, to ensure your health and well-being. And as for the sun's magical properties, its healing rays can cleanse and recharge your spiritual centre, especially when you focus on this aspect as part of a sun meditation. (Always take care to protect yourself if planning to spend any extended amount of time exposed to the sun.)

You will need:
- A quiet place outdoors to sit where you can feel the sun on your face and body

Practising the meditation:
Once you've found a sunny, peaceful spot, settle into a comfortable seated position (this can be a classic lotus position or anything else that you're happy with).

Focus on your breathing, noticing the sensation of softly exhaling and inhaling. As you're concentrating on this, let your mind clear of any distracting thoughts.

As you feel the warming rays of the sun on your face and body, imagine a bright white light radiating from your heart and connecting with the glow of the sun. Mediate on this image for as long as you feel comfortable.

When you feel ready, open your eyes and thank the sun for its blessing.

FOR ADDED MAGIC…

Burn a yellow candle in a fireproof bowl while meditating to enhance the effect of bright solar energy.

Healing plants and herbs

Folklore and folk magic are no more aligned than when it comes to the power of medicinal herbs. Knowledge of the healing properties of flowers, plants, trees and fruit available locally was of great benefit to the average person at a time when pharmaceutical medicine had not even been conceived of. Knowing that birch bark could help ease inflammation and accelerate the healing of a wound or that camomile could help aid sleep would have been invaluable. And if you didn't have this kind of knowledge, you could consult your local cunning man or woman for practical remedies and various means of spiritual restoration.

Aside from their various magical associations, some of which we have already explored, many common flora found in Europe are central to folklore traditions:

Elder – Celtic lore suggests that if you stand under this fruit-bearing tree on Midsummer's Eve, you will see the king of the fairies and his merry troupe ride by, while English lore says that if someone who has been baptized were to smear the juice from elderberries around their eyes, they would be able to identify a witch.

Rosemary – certain cultures hold that if you place a sprig of this richly scented herb in your hair, your memory will improve, whereas placing it under your pillow at night will help ward off bad dreams.

Sage – aside from its use in Native American smudging ceremonies, this deeply fragrant herb was also used by some indigenous communities as a means of cleaning their teeth and gums. It is also believed to be a cure for warts.

Thyme – this sweet herb, when burned, is said to clear your house of insects. If you're keen to attract fairies into your garden, cultivate a bed of thyme, which they apparently favour as a resting place.

Lucky Charms

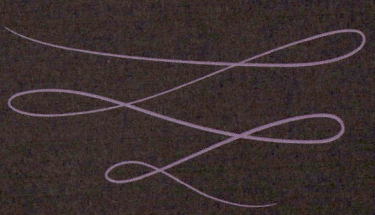

Many people throughout history have interpreted luck in terms of inexplicable blessings or curses that arrive at our doorstep like a feather blown in the wind. Good luck is cheerily welcomed as an unexpected stroke of positive fortune, while bad luck is bitterly lamented as an unfair punishment at the hands of fate or perhaps an angry deity. Magic tries to encourage a view that does away with this kind of diametric. Happenstance is not directed by some hidden vindictive force or benevolent spirit but is simply a window of transition, a shift in energies that, if recognized as such, can be connected with and used as a means for constructive change. Lucky charms are a little reminder of this concept – a way to achieve a mindset that sees fortune of all kinds as an opportunity for learning and renewed focus.

*A wise man turns chance
into good fortune.*

THOMAS FULLER

AMOR FATI

(LOVE YOUR FATE)

A rowan-berry necklace for protection

The rowan tree, which in autumn is replete with bunches of bright red berries, has various long-established magical and mythological connections. In Celtic mythology in particular, the tree is regarded as portal to the spirit world. Even early Christians adopted rowan-twig charms as a way of warding off evil spirits, as did farmers who hung a rowan cross tied with red thread above the barn door to ensure their herd would not be harmed. With all of the magical weight behind it, a rowan-berry necklace is the perfect thing for protection against negative energy and misfortune.

You will need:

- A dozen or so dried rowan berries
- A heavy-gauge needle
- Red embroidery thread or wool
- A cord or thong to serve as the main part of your necklace (measure a length that will allow the charm to sit where you're happy with it, then subtract 15 cm (6 in.) from that length)

Making the charm:

If you're foraging for your own berries, be mindful to only take a few and give thanks to the tree as you pick

them. Leave them in a cool, dry place to harden for around two weeks. It is also possible to acquire them ready-dried online.

Take a 15-cm (6-in.) length of thread and attach it to your needle.

Pick up your first berry, push the needle through the centre and out the other side so the thread runs through the berry. Push the berry down to the end of the thread and repeat with the rest.

Once you have your berries threaded, tie the ends of the thread to the ends of your cord/thong securely to create a necklace.

A daisy-wheel charm for protection

Magic is full of symbols, from the unmistakable pentacle (the encircled, five-pointed star, itself a talisman for protection) to the triple moon, a circle nestled between two crescents. They serve as a pictorial embodiment of a particular power or intent, and the simplistic nature of their form makes them ideal for everyday folk-magic practitioners. The daisy wheel, a six-petalled "flower" within a circle, also known as a "witch mark", has been observed through history notched into timbers near the threshold of buildings to ensure evil spirits could not enter. The circle may represent the sun, an eternal source of life and renewal, and the flower itself may also tie into creative energy and joyful rebirth.

You will need:

- A drawing compass
- A pen, pencil or piece of chalk (depending on where you are applying your mark, i.e. on paper to carry on your person or on wood/brick to protect a threshold)

Making the charm:

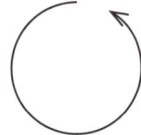

1   First, draw a circle.

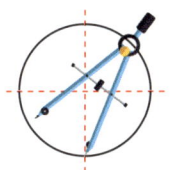

2   Place the compass point on the outer part of the circle directly below the centre point.

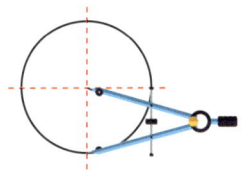

3   Set the pen or pencil to intersect with the centre point.

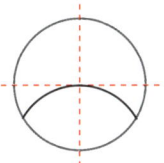

4   Draw an arc from edge to edge.

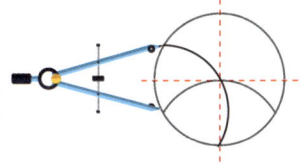

5   Next, place the compass at the left-hand point where your first arc intersects with the circle and draw another arc, edge to edge.

6   Continue in this way, clockwise, until you have your six-petalled daisy.

A lemon pig for a New-Year blessing

Practically all cultures around the world have customs related to the "new year, new you" concept, ranging from eating lucky raisins (Spain and Portugal) to throwing a bucket of dirty water out of the front door to signify the common "out with the old, in with the new" sentiment (Cuba). The lemon pig, first mentioned in an American publication in the mid 1800s, is a curious and cute way of blessing your home for the new year.

You will need:

- A lemon
- Four matchsticks or cocktail sticks
- Two whole cloves
- A paring knife
- A small square of tinfoil
- A coin

Making the charm:

Select an end for the pig's head and create two ears by slicing two small flaps into the rind, bending them upwards.

Cut a slice a little deeper below the "nose" on the head end, for the mouth. Check to see that the coin will fit inside and stay put. Adjust as necessary.

Insert two cloves into the lemon for your pig's eyes.

Push in the four matchsticks/cocktail sticks for the pig's legs.

Take the tinfoil square and pinch it in the middle, twisting it until you have a curly tail with a flap at the end, which should be used to scrunch around the rear of the pig.

Place the finished pig in a prominent place in the house to remind you that prosperity is just around the corner!

The lucky horseshoe

In the Western world, there can hardly be a more familiar symbol of good luck than the horseshoe. Countless inns, barns and stables across the UK and North America are decorated with horseshoes, not simply to display an equestrian interest but to bless the properties they adorn. But what possible association could a metal crescent used to protect the hooves of horses have with good fortune?

Like many magical objects and practices, there are numerous ideas behind the origin. The closest thing to a scholarly treatise on the subject can be found in Robert Means Lawrence's *The Magic of the Horse-Shoe*, published in 1898. This remarkable volume covers various possible sources of the horseshoe's magic power in great detail. One theory advanced by Lawrence is the tale of "St Dunstan and the Devil". Aside from his involvement

with the Church (he would eventually rise to become the Archbishop of Canterbury), Dunstan was a skilled blacksmith. According to the legend, one day the Devil, disguised as a traveller, appeared at Dunstan's forge, asking for one of the shoes on his horse to be replaced. Dunstan saw through the Devil's disguise and somehow tricked him into getting his own hoof shod, which caused Old Nick so much pain that he begged for the smith to cease. Dunstan's condition was that the Devil could never cross the threshold of a property with a horseshoe above the door.

Other theories surmise that horseshoes were once made of iron, which in some lore can repel evil spirits, while others suggest that the shoe's crescent shape connects it to the moon and thus it carries the blessings of the goddess thereof.

An acorn keyring for positive energy

In Norse mythology, the oak tree is associated with Thor, god of thunder and lightning. The acorn, then, encapsulates this godly favour, as well as being a simple, natural symbol of potential: as Chaucer said, "Mighty oaks from little acorns grow," so carrying one with you is a reminder that you too are full of powerful prospects.

You will need:

- A brown acorn
- A skewer or a drill with a small-gauge bit
- A short length of thong or sturdy twine – about 8 cm (3 in.)

Making the charm:

Select a drill bit or skewer that will create a hole wide enough for the thong or twine to pass through and bore through your acorn.

Thread the fastening through the hole and attach the charm to something you carry with you every day, such as the keys for your house or car.

FOR ADDED MAGIC…

Before making your charm, place the acorn on your windowsill in the light of a full moon, where it will draw in positive, good-luck energy.

A horned hand to banish negativity

In mainstream Anglo-centric culture, the horned hand – a sign made with one's forefinger and little finger extended and the remaining fingers clenched in a fist – has come to be regarded as satanic, often tied in with heavy metal music. However, if one were to visit Italy, one might well encounter this symbol in a diametrical context. The *mano cornuta* (horned hand) in Italian folk belief is a symbol of protection against the evil eye, i.e. spiritual malevolence. Aside from being a gesture that can be directed at anyone suspected of trying to cast negativity your way, horned hands have long been crafted into charms made of precious materials, such as mother-of-pearl, silver, gold or coral. The latter material offers the opportunity for the hand to be coloured red, which adds an extra layer of luck.

You will need:

- Dextrous fingers (or, if you don't plan on performing the gesture, a way of acquiring a manufactured charm)

Using the charm:

Although the gesture is familiar to metalheads the world over, and you're very likely to see it thrust up into the air at a live show, outside of this it's very much rooted in Italian culture. The physical charm, which can be added to a bracelet or hung in a car to ensure safe passage, is a less personal expression of the sentiment that seems to have been more widely adopted and commodified.

A charmed corsage for protection

In folk magic, the uses of local flora are almost inexhaustible, and they can be employed in a ritualistic context as well as in potions and tinctures. One of the simplest ways to benefit from the power of plant magic is to keep them on your person, and what better way than with a humble corsage? We perhaps most associate this practice with formal occasions such as weddings, where the bride and groom will use them purely as an attractive adornment, but it actually dates back to ancient Greece, when small bunches of flowers and herbs were worn to ward off evil spirits.

You will need:

- Any combination of the following herbs and flowers, using a sprig of fresh or a pinch of dried:
  - Valerian, primrose, peppermint – for happiness in relationships
  - Fennel, tarragon, pennyroyal – for inner strength
- Red clover, bergamot, heather – for luck
- Thyme, bay, basil – for success in business
- Camomile, lavender, oregano – for health
- Oregano, marjoram, citronella – for happiness

- Lemon balm, rose, jasmine – for love
- Scissors
- Some (ideally red) thread or wool
- A pin to affix the corsage to your clothing (optional)

Making the charm:

Decide how large you want your corsage to be – 10 cm (4 in.) is a practical size if you're attaching it to your clothing.

Taking the flowers and herbs, remove leaves, if necessary, so you have a clear couple of centimetres at the bottom of all stems.

Trim the stems for a nice, even finish.

Arrange the stems into an attractive bunch and tie them together with the thread/wool.

A pig for luck

Across Europe, and especially in Germany, the humble pig has long been regarded as something of a lucky charm. Unlike the lemon pig (see page 112), which by comparison seems like a bit of frivolous fun, the role of the pig – or, more specifically, pork – is significant. Before the age of modern conveniences, a family with a pig was considered blessed, since they were guaranteed a hearty meal at a time when food could be scarce. Though society largely moved away from keeping animals for food, the sentiment stuck, and people wishing others well began to present each other with stand-in swine: ones made of marzipan or illustrated on greetings cards. Here we suggest making a painted modelling-clay pig to bless a friend or family member with.

You will need:
- A block of air-drying modelling clay
- A set of acrylic paints

Making the charm:
How you choose to shape your pig is up to you, whether it be just a smiling face or a full-body design.

According to the packet instructions, prepare and shape your modelling clay into a piggy masterpiece.

Next, break out your paints and embellish the features.

Leave to dry for at least 48 hours before gifting.

FOR ADDED MAGIC…

Drill a hole large enough to pass a red or green ribbon through, to maximize the luck-attracting potential of your lucky pig.

A charm in a bottle for protection

One of the most personal – and potentially most powerful – written charms is one of your own devising. Magic is generally made up of guidelines and established practices, but folk magic stands out as being far less doctrinal and therefore, in many ways, naive. But this naiveté is really a kind of honesty – the intent behind the magic is simple and pure, not complicated by endlessly specific requirements. Hence, a written charm scribed with heart, sealed safely inside a bottle and secreted on a property you wish to protect is as pure and simple as it gets.

You will need:
- A piece of paper
- A pen
- A glass bottle that can be sealed

Making the charm:
Choose a quiet spot to write your charm.

Focus your intent by reciting your wishes for protection in your mind.

Once you feel you have them clear, write them down on the paper using whatever words feel right to you.

Roll up the paper, place it inside your bottle and hide it in a spot where it can't be disturbed.

If you wish to follow a historical lead on the phrasing of your charm, consider the following from 1882:

Sun, Moon, Mars, Mercury, Jupiter, Venus, Saturn, Trine, Sextile, Dragon's Head, Dragon's Tail; I charge you to guard this house from all evil spirits whatever, and guard it from all disorders, and from anything being taken wrongly, and give this family good health and wealth.

The four-leaf clover

A strong contender for the most universally recognized good-luck symbol is the four-leaf clover, which has embedded itself deeply into mainstream awareness and popular culture. It's been adopted in cereals (Lucky Charms) and by football teams (Celtic FC), car companies (Alfa Romeo's racing models) and various European organizations and political parties. It is often mistakenly associated with Ireland, whose national symbol is the three-leaf shamrock (though, of course, clovers with all numbers of leaves grow in Ireland).

Its status as a good-luck charm is, as ever, somewhat multifaceted, but it was mentioned in this context as early as 1620, in a play by Englishman Sir John Melton, who wrote, "That if a man walking in the fields, finde any foure-leaued grasse, he shall in small while after finde some good thing." Clovers are classed botanically as trefoils, meaning three-leaved, so while the plant is to be found in many places throughout the world, to come across one with four leaves is indeed something of a relative rarity. Some estimates say that the chance is 1 in 10,000.

As for their magical significance, they are generally regarded as an all-round enhancer of positive energy and good fortune – a charm of charms, if you will. Some people break the leaves down into four sentiments – hope, faith, love and good fortune – while others hold that acquiring a four-leaf clover could grant the ability to see fairies.

The clover's capacities are seemingly endless, but it is certainly fitting that arguably the most potent folk magic symbol of all is a humble legume that is common in gardens and on pastures and hillsides across the world.

Folk Celebrations and Festivals

Although they might seem quaint and curious to anyone unfamiliar with them, folk traditions offer a direct window into our magical past. While superstition and arguably "unenlightened" beliefs play a part, at its heart this past is most often defined by an intimate relationship with nature – be it knowledge of the local flora and fauna and the cycles of the moon or a healthy respect for the power of the elements. Folkloric festivals and rituals are always seasonal and, while their peculiarities might seem eccentric, they all have a specific purpose that at one time would have been of great cultural importance. Thankfully, the value of folk traditions is once again being recognized, and this chapter offers just some of the many historic practices that are being kept alive by people today.

*It takes an endless amount of history
to make even a little tradition.*

HENRY JAMES

OPEN YOUR EYES TO THE WONDER OF THE OLD WAYS

Beltane blazes and a leafy green May in the UK

There is much activity in the folkloric calendar in the spring. After the dreary hardship of winter, where in many countries the days are dark and cold, nature begins to wake up and burst into life. Renewal and reinvigoration are central to many festivals around this time, and few are more spectacular than the Beltane Fire Festival in Edinburgh, Scotland. "Beltane" roughly translates as "bright fire" and the Beltane ritual harks back to an ancient Gaelic celebration that took place on the evening of 30 April to mark the arrival of summer. The summer sun brings its own fire, of course, but a Beltane bonfire was lit to signify the cleansing transition from darkness and decay to light and life. Participants in the ritual would dance around the fire and leap across it to purify themselves. Today's event in Edinburgh naturally includes a bonfire but also features a grand procession led by folk characters who will be familiar to many in Europe: the May Queen and the Green Man.

While the Green Man has a shared billing at Beltane, he's the sole star of the show at the Jack in the Green festival in Hastings, England. As you might guess from his moniker, the Green Man is, essentially, the spirit of nature, often depicted with a green face surrounded by a wreath of leaves sprouting from his head and beard, and sometimes with tendrils emerging from his mouth. His presence marks the onset, once again, of new life, and in his guise at Hastings he is seen in full leafy glory – a flowery crown atop his head, trailing coloured ribbons, and covered head to foot in evergreen leaves, looking as if a tree had sprouted legs and decided to parade through the town. To release the spirit of summer, though, he must be slain, which forms the finale of the festival on top of West Hill.

Dancing for the dead and appeasing the god of disaster in Japan

Modern Japanese culture is replete with ancient customs that play a significant role in the national identity. Among the many traditional celebrations throughout the year is the Obon festival, which occurs most typically in August and is based on the Buddhist idea of acknowledging and celebrating the spirits of one's ancestors (though ancestor veneration existed in Japanese culture before the arrival of Buddhism). Aside from tending to shrines dedicated to their loved ones, celebrants can observe the spectacle of the *bon odori*, a joyful folk dance, performed on a raised wooden platform, consisting of simple swaying and clapping movements, often to the percussive sound of traditional Japanese *min'yō* music. As with many folk customs, the celebration has many region-specific variations, some including decorative fans or towels and folk instruments such as *kachi kachi* (wooden castanets).

The Gion Matsuri is a month-long festival that takes place in Tokyo in July. As with many folk practices, it was born out of necessity. In the ninth century, Tokyo suffered from an epidemic believed to be caused by vengeful spirits. In an attempt to appeal for aid from Susanoo-no-Mikoto, the storm god, Emperor Seiwa ordered a purification ritual to be performed, featuring no less than 66 decorated halberds (staff-like weapons). This ritual was repeated each time an outbreak occurred, eventually becoming an annual event. The traditional halberds evolved into elaborate, towering rope-and-timber floats in the shape of ships and buildings, which are hauled through the streets on wooden wheels by fleets of people in formal dress. Although today the Gion Matsuri is a sprawling celebration, its origins are still remembered: each year a local boy is chosen to act as a sacred messenger to the gods. For the four days between 13 and 17 July he is transported aboard one of the floats, ensuring his feet don't touch the ground!

Guardians of the night in West Africa

Vodún (the inspiration for the more modern offshoots of vodou and voodoo), an eclectic and adaptive religion practised across West Africa, is essentially defined by the worship of various spirits that govern different aspects of nature and society, often with a given sect dedicated to a particular divinity. The city of Ouidah, in Benin, home of the Temple of Pythons, populated by 60 sacred snakes, is the site of the most prominent festival celebrating this belief system. Each year in January, factions from across the land gather to affirm and showcase their specific practices, with some dressing as Zangbeto – spirit guardians of the night who roam the streets in search of wrongdoers. Enveloped head to toe in a mass of hay or palm fibres, at the top of which might be a stoic-looking mask, believers enter a trance in order to embody the very spirit they are giving praise to.

VODÚN FETISHES

The term "fetish" might sound somewhat out of place in a discussion about sacred beliefs, but it is in fact derived from the Latin *facere*, "to make". In the context of Vodún, the objects created are folkloric to the core: material representations of a spirit (or objects related to the spirit) made from wood, stone, shell or bone, which can be carried as a protective talisman or used in a ritual evoking said divinity. Fetishes can range from carved phalluses to preserved animal heads – anything that can be sourced locally. These objects, along with sacred herbal preparations, are also linked to healing. A Vodún priest, much the same as the cunning person or shaman, can offer spiritual and physical remedies – at a price.

Tailless pigs and skeletal horses in Wales

It might not be surprising to discover that in Wales, where the national flag features a mythical beast (a red dragon), folkloric traditions are thriving. Like many of the realms of Britannia, Wales has connections with Arthurian legend, but the Welsh people have always been proud to weave the threads of their own unique and authentic narrative. One such thread can be found in Nos Calan Gaeaf (Winter's Eve), the night before the first day of winter (1 November). On this night, known as an Ysbrydnos or "spirit night", it is supposed that spirits roam the Earth. Tradition dictates that people avoid churchyards, stiles and crossroads lest they encounter one of these ghostly forms. And it's not just wandering spirits they need to look out for. As part of the Nos Calan Gaeaf tradition, a bonfire is lit and, as it begins to die down, children are invited to write their

name on a stone and cast it into the embers. They return the next day and if they succeed in finding their stone, they will have good luck for the coming year. However, there is a catch – if they linger too long as the fire is dying, their soul could be gobbled up by the terrible tailless black sow Hwch Ddu Gwta!

The animal-themed antagonism doesn't end there. Around Christmastime in South Wales, one can expect a visit from a ghostly horse with a skinless head, Mari Lwyd. This is part of a wassailing tradition (performing for the reward of food and ale) in which a band of costumed folk characters, accompanied by the disturbing hobby horse (a horse skull, or mock skull, on the end of a pole, with the operator covered by a white sheet), would go door to door, appealing to residents for some form of nourishment. Yes, just like Halloween!

Buttery pancakes and a blazing wicker woman in Russia

Although Russia is often associated with the Orthodox Church, traces of its pagan roots can still be found. Indeed, in the case of Maslenitsa, occurring around late winter/early spring, the two orders seem to have merged. In the build-up to Lent, many Christian traditions involve a period of indulgence and merriment, and this is the case with "Butter Week", a colloquial name for Maslenitsa in which dairy products are consumed with abandon, often in the form of *blini* (pancakes), since for those who follow the custom devoutly, they are not permitted again until Easter. Not only do celebrants get to indulge their taste for dairy, but they are also given leave from work to engage in social activities and dancing before Lent commences.

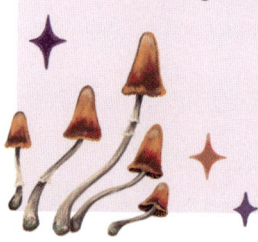

Maslenitsa is also known as Babskyi Tyzhden, which translates as "Women's Week". Between eating and drinking, married women were once encouraged to confirm their union by burying a wooden log, while unfortunate singletons had their logs tied to their leg, presumably so they could literally carry the weight of their failure to find a suitable partner. By far the most divergent aspect of this time, though, is the burning of the Lady Maslenitsa effigy. This brightly dressed figure, with a sunny visage (sometimes literally made with the face of a cartoonish sun) is set ablaze in a tradition related to ensuring a bountiful harvest and to mark the end of winter. The effigy is a lady because the word for "winter" in Russian is feminine, and once she has been rendered to ashes her remains are scooped up and buried in the snow to "fertilize the crops" of the coming harvest season, be that literally or metaphorically.

A child-stealing anti-Claus in Germany

It will be no surprise to learn that the nation that inspired Jacob and Wilhelm Grimm, responsible for probably the most well-known and celebrated collection of fairy tales in the West, is full of folkloric traditions and characters. One such figure, fully in keeping with the sinister tone of the Grimm tales, is that of Krampus: a terrifying goat-demon who is, as unbelievable as it sounds, a henchman and counterpart to the venerable Saint Nicholas. Saint Nick is, of course, one of the main inspirations for that most cheerful and charitable of all make-believe holiday mascots, Santa Claus. So, what on earth is he doing hanging around with an evil horned demon carrying a sack and a birchwood whip?!

The basic premise is that while Saint Nicholas will bless and reward those children who have been well behaved, Krampus would punish those who had not. This might involve a stern thrashing with the whip or, if they had been especially bad, full-blown kidnapping.

This night of horrific judgement occurs on 5 December, the day before the feast of Saint Nicholas. So, if you thought being on Santa's naughty list was as bad as it gets, spare a thought for all the poor German children who have faced the wrath of the hairy Christmas Devil, Krampus!

THE AUSTRIAN KRAMPUSNACHT PARADE

While Krampus seems to be more of a fairy tale than a folk tradition, there are some who have taken it upon themselves to bring the terror to life. Each year in the Austrian state of Tyrol, towns and cities across the region indulge in elaborate Krampusnacht parades involving processions of suitably raucous costumed Krampuses heartily snarling and spooking the kiddies in only the most traditionally wicked fashion. Attend if you dare – but only if you've been good!

Flying oranges and a donkey derby in Italy

The history of Italy tells of many famous military battles, but none can rival the juicy drama of the famous Battaglia delle Arance (Battle of the Oranges), which takes place in February in the city of Ivrea in Northern Italy as part of the Carnevale di Ivrea. The object is to recount the folk history behind the dethroning of the malevolent Duke Guido III, who attempted to force himself upon a local miller's daughter but who ended up being beheaded as a result, sparking an all-out revolution in the city and a violent clash between the populace and the duke's army. These two factions are represented by two teams of *aranceri* (orange handlers) in the food fight. The defenders are made up of nine squadrons representing the nine original districts of the town, each with their own medieval-style jerseys emblazoned with a logo. Their job is to pelt the duke's tyrants,

who are set up in raised carts. How rules can be enforced or a winner decided upon in a food fight is anyone's guess!

Yet another conflict is the inspiration for the Palio degli Asini (donkey race) in Alba, another location in Northern Italy. The historical premise this time is that, in 1275, people from a rival town (Asti) launched a surprise attack on the vineyards at Alba, devastating the crop. To rub salt into the wound, some of the assailants flexed their muscles by galloping their horses around the town walls. As a form of parodic revenge, the folk of Alba staged a riding display of their own, undermining the prowess of the Asti riders by charging around on diminutive donkeys. In honour of their past defiance, Alba holds a *palio* each year in October.

Woven rainbow masks and mountain gods in South America

As with many of the most ancient folk rituals across the world, celebrating the sun, giver of light and life, is central to the Inti Raymi festival in Peru and Ecuador, held in late June. The winter solstice – the shortest day of the year in terms of sunlight – marks the Incan New Year, when the days will begin to draw out and the sun will have its season once again. The original festival lasted for nine days and involved dances, colourful costumes, feasting and animal sacrifice – all of which the Spanish Catholic colonizers thought was far too pagan to be permitted. The last celebration before the arrival of the Spanish was in 1535, but thankfully it was revived several hundred years later in 1944. Today, the festival is both a celebration and a historical re-enactment with period costumes, featuring the delightful *aya huma* mask: a multicoloured woven/knitted face covering with a

visage front and back, tongue protruding, worn to represent a protective force that will drive away evil spirits during the ceremony.

Yet another event that was disapproved of by the Church was the Carnaval de Oruro, now held in Bolivia in early February. Because of the Catholic influence, today the festival is essentially an Easter event, but the original purpose was to mark a pilgrimage to the Sacred Mountain of the Urus where various deities reside, such as Jamp'atu Qullu (the hill toad) and Quwak (the viper). A showcase of folk dances is now the main focus, with participants from numerous local regions dressed in elaborate, embellished costumes representing a kaleidoscope of styles. Indeed, the spectacle is so impressive that it has been deemed one of the Masterpieces of the Oral and Intangible Heritage of Humanity, as defined by UNESCO.

Stormy portents and loving trinkets in Romania

March can be a tense time for women who choose to follow the tradition linked with Babele, which refers to the first nine days of the month, when they are likely to be looking forward to the oncoming joys of spring. However, if luck – or, more specifically, the weather – isn't on their side, then the next year might not be so joyous after all. According to the tradition, one of the first nine days of March is chosen to be an indicator for the rest of the year. If they choose a day when the sun shines, a blessed and fruitful year lies ahead. However, if they select a day that's cold or rainy then, sadly, their year will be tumultuous. The reason for the nine-day window lies in the tale of Baba Dochia, a shepherdess who made a poorly timed trip out into the mountains where – because she had misjudged the weather – she froze to death. It is told that she died on the ninth day after she set out.

In a custom that somewhat resembles Valentine's Day, Martisor, the gifting of *martisorul* (trinkets), most usually from men to women as a show of affection and respect, also takes place in March. Whether the present-giver chooses a handmade flower, some jewellery or a pair of woven dollies, each gift must display a red-and-white-striped cord. The colours have particular relevance to the time of year: the red represents the warmth of the sun, while the white represents the frosty cold. Recipients sometimes choose to wear their *martisorul* throughout March, believing it to be good luck, whereas others, on the last day of the month, tie the cord to a fruit tree, which is said to bring wealth.

Traditional dress and a gift-bearing goat in Finland

Finland might well be the most folkloric place on Earth, with its tales of trolls and mermaids, fairies, sprites and elves, and a calendar full of traditional celebrations. One might say that folklore is woven into the very fabric of the nation – and indeed that is the case in terms of their national dress, Kansallispuku, which comprises intricately embroidered vests (*liivi*), skirts and kilts, and often decorative headwear known as *päähine*. This costume, often sported by participants during one of the many historic celebrations held annually, paints a perfect picture of the vibrancy and uniqueness of Finnish custom.

Everybody knows that Santa Claus lives in Finland, but not all may be familiar with the

joulupukki, the Christmas goat. It would be more accurate to describe this mysterious beast as a Yule goat, since it's not connected in any way to the religious event. In the pagan conception, it was understood to be a malevolent spirit that, rather than visit people's houses to bestow gifts upon them, would demand a portion of the Yule feast! In time, Christian influence inspired a merging of ideas, conflating *joulupukki* with Old Saint Nick – an old goat, to be sure, but no longer in the literal sense. Gladly, in some parts of Finland the Yule goat survives through seasonal costumed performances – interestingly, most often by older men – in exchange for a festive treat. Whether or not the Yule goat is a mean spirit, a gift-bearing sidekick or Santa himself, the motif has survived in Finland and across Scandinavia, making the season of goodwill a little more folky and interesting.

Conclusion

Hopefully, on your journey through the wondrous landscape of folk magic, your eyes have been opened to the notion that even the most mundane and familiar of objects, the most ordinary habit or humble half-belief, can be conceived of as something with a value much greater than is apparent at first glance: that these everyday things can be magical. This, after all, is the true value of folklore and folk traditions. Tall tales of fantastical beings and old-fashioned cultural curiosities have a place as a means of quaint fascination, but what they really offer is an inspiring connection to a past that was infinitely more in touch with nature and, perhaps even more importantly, wonder.

This kind of magical understanding offers so much scope for enlightenment, healing and joy, and a way of balancing out the constant demands and pressures of

modern life. That lucky charm you carried to your big interview or the spell you cast for healing or protection might not have any discernible material effect, but it could help you see the potential or solution that was already there waiting.

Many of the magical methods offered in this book have been directly inspired by tried-and-tested practices that have been galvanized by decades if not centuries of history. However, this should not preclude you from establishing your own approaches. There is always room for new ways to emerge, for new tales to be written and for new traditions to be forged. Keep this in mind as you navigate your own magical path, and it is bound to lead to an inspiring and blessed destination.

Notes

LOVE MAGIC

Lydia Levine

Hardback

978-1-83799-689-6

See your passion soar to new heights with this enchanting guide to love magic, potions and spellwork

This little book is the perfect introduction to using magic to enrich your relationships, both amorous and platonic. Whether you're looking to harness your most romantic self, manifest what you most desire or create long-lasting relationships, this book has the spell for you. Who knows – the secret to eternal happiness may be just a spell away.

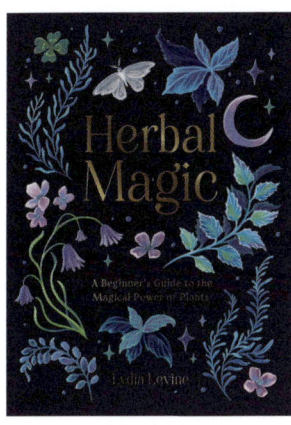

HERBAL MAGIC

Lydia Levine

Hardback

978-1-83799-129-7

Step into the enchanting world of herbal recipes, remedies and rituals with this spellbinding guide to the magical power of plants

This treasury of herb profiles is the perfect introduction to conjuring your inner power and enriching your life with a little herbal magic. Whether you are drawn to blends and brews or elixirs and potions, the unique natural powers of these bewitching ingredients are ready and waiting for you.

Have you enjoyed this book? If so, find us on Facebook at **Summersdale Publishers**, on Twitter/X at **@Summersdale** and on Instagram, TikTok and Bluesky at **@summersdalebooks** and get in touch. We'd love to hear from you!

www.summersdale.com

Image credits

Watercolour illustrations by Marianne Thompson; pp.3, 4–5, 20–21, 30–31, 68–69, 90–91, 102–103, 126–127, 132–133, 136–137, 138–139, 142–143, 144–145, 148–149, 150–151, 152–153, 154–157 © Mio Buono/Shutterstock.com; p.13 © Elfe 360/Shutterstock.com; p.15 © TLpixs/Shutterstock.com; p.17 © Jelena990/Shutterstock.com; p.19 © JurateBuiviene/Shutterstock.com; p.23 © Natalia Klenova/Shutterstock.com; p.25 © Siarhei Zuyonak/Shutterstock.com; p.27 © New Africa/Shutterstock.com; p.29 © Wirestock Creators/Shutterstock.com; p.37 © banu sevim/Shutterstock.com; p.39 © Violeta Beigiene/Shutterstock.com; p.41 © ju_see/Shutterstock.com; p.43 © ganjalex/Shutterstock.com; p.45 © Leigh Prather/Shutterstock.com; p.47 © Henk Vrieselaar/Shutterstock.com; p.51 © TabitaZn/Shutterstock.com; p.53 © Marben/Shutterstock.com; p.61 © AVN Photo Lab/Shutterstock.com; p.63 © SarahLou Photography/Shutterstock.com; p.65 © Zwickie/Shutterstock.com; p.67 © zef art/Shutterstock.com; p.71 © Witaya Proadtayakogool/Shutterstock.com; p.73 © Klymenko Mariia/Shutterstock.com; p.75 © nutsiam/Shutterstock.com; p.77 © Phototribe/Shutterstock.com; p.85 © Pasko Maksim/Shutterstock.com; p.87 © FotoHelin/Shutterstock.com; p.89 © Stanislav_63/Shutterstock.com; p.93 © FotoHelin/Shutterstock.com; p.97 © sripfoto/Shutterstock.com; p.99 © NDanko/Shutterstock.com; p.101 © Akarawut/Shutterstock.com; p.109 © Wirestock Creators/Shutterstock.com; p.111 – compass © RealVector/Shutterstock.com; p.113 photo by Chris Turton; p.117 © 912038419009842/Shutterstock.com; p.119 © Sodel Vladyslav/Shutterstock.com; p.121 © natalia bulatova/Shutterstock.com; p.123 © Nicole Lienemann/Shutterstock.com; p.125 © n_defender/Shutterstock.com